The Use of Official Statistics in Sociology

A Critique of Positivism and Ethnomethodology

BARRY HINDESS

Lecturer in Social Statistics, University of Liverpool

Macmillan

First published 1973 by
THE MACMILLAN PRESS LTD
London and Basingstoke
Associated companies in New York Dublin
Melbourne Johannesburg and Madras

SBN 333 13772 8

Printed in Great Britain by
THE ANCHOR PRESS LTD
Tiptree, Essex

CONTENTS

ACKNOWLEDGEMENTS

Many individuals have read and commented upon early drafts of parts of this study. I am particularly grateful to Gary Littlejohn for his many critical remarks and helpful suggestions and also to the editor of this series for his critical reading of the first complete draft.

1. INTRODUCTION

THE chaotic and frequently incoherent state of modern sociology, reflected in its theoretical anarchy and the coexistence within it of radically heterogeneous and often incompatible positions, is now widely recognised and commonly deplored. Particularly disturbing in the present situation is that so many recent works in sociological theory and especially, but not only, in the field of deviance have developed an essentially anti-theoretical critique of the forms of proof and types of evidence used by their theoretical opponents. This tendency, which opposes concepts and rationalist forms of demonstration to human 'experience' as the foundation of knowledge, is by no means new but is carried to an extreme in modern forms of ethnomethodology and social phenomenology.[1] The present text makes no attempt to examine the generality of these positions. Rather, perhaps less ambitiously, it considers recent critiques directed particularly against the use of certain types of evidence in the social sciences. By examining the ways in which materials are collected and aggregated into official statistics, they appear to show that these – and social statistics in general – cannot be taken to represent, more or less accurately, some real state of affairs. Their authors' strictures with regard to sociologists' use of official statistics derive from a more general theoretical concern. Thus, Cicourel is 'concerned with the development of methods (which I view as basic to theory construction) for particular theoretical issues', while Douglas' arguments are 'directed at what seems to me to be the fundamental problems of sociology'[2] ([13] p. vii, and [14]

[1] For a critique of one important source of these positions see [23]. (References in square brackets refer to works listed in the Bibliography, pp. 59–63 below.)

[2] I refer primarily to these authors rather than to the texts of Garfinkel and Schutz (see Bibliography), upon which they clearly depend. This is because they both provide extensive and elaborated critiques of the use of certain types of statistics in sociology.

p. 338). While this study is primarily concerned with the evaluation and possible usefulness of statistical materials for scientific purposes, it will be necessary to argue that these are empty claims and that no theoretical problems of any substance are raised by their arguments.

Unfortunately the vulgar positivism of what these authors call 'orthodox' methodology is such as to invite precisely the type of argument that we must consider. For this positivism, as for its phenomenological and ethnomethodological opponents, knowledge is founded upon the experience of a human subject. There is a world of facts that may be unequivocally described in a series of elementary propositions, each of which refers to the irreducible elements of experience. This position is discussed in the Appendix. Here it is sufficient to note that contemporary variants of positivism normally distinguish between 'observational' and 'theoretical' terms and languages. The former are said to be pre-theoretical (i.e. independent of any theory) and are used to refer to 'observable' things and events and to their 'observable' properties. The latter refers to theoretical constructs related in a more or less complex fashion to the observational terms. The function of this distinction in methodological discourse and its profound inadequacies will be examined in the Appendix.

In the texts of 'orthodox' methodology the existence of an intersubjectively valid observation language is assumed. Descriptions in this language provide a firm basis against which theories and hypotheses may be tested. The critique that social phenomenology and ethnomethodology direct against the use of official statistics appears to ask only that this intersubjective validity be demonstrated. Thus, in spite of certain differences of emphasis, it is argued that any observer must utilise 'tacit knowledge' or 'background expectancies' in the identification and selection of materials from his environment to be recorded as 'what happened', as the observed objects of events. Consequently, if the 'observer's remarks are not to be taken on faith as an accurate portrayal of "what happened" ' ([13] p. 6), it is necessary that we be informed of the mode of functioning of these background expectancies or this tacit knowledge.

In addition, it is held, official statistics are assembled by bureaucratic apparatuses, which process the initial observers' reports through a whole series of modifications and transformations to

10

produce the final tabulated results. It follows, for example, that census materials cannot be taken 'as adequate descriptions of specifiable phenomena' ([13] p. 2). Rather they are the product of the observed events, the background expectancies of the observers, and of the processing of the observers' reports by bureaucratic apparatuses.

The necessary relativism and agnosticism of these positions may be simply indicated. (It will be elaborated at length below.) The basic methodological problem in respect of observation is said to be as follows :

Unless the respondent's and the researcher's decoding and encoding procedures are basic elements of the research enterprise, we cannot make sense of either the phenomena being studied or the materials labelled 'findings'.

To get around this difficulty Cicourel suggests that

in analysing conversations and reports, the researcher must approximate a 're-writing' of the dialogue or prose so that he can communicate the unstated and seen but unnoticed background expectancies for the reader. Such a procedure would enable the reader to understand how the participants and observer made sense of their environment as portrayed by the researcher ([13] p. 3 and p. 18).

Douglas, on the other hand, criticises sociologists for their reliance upon observers' descriptions and classifications of phenomena and calls instead for 'careful descriptions of real-world events' ([14] p. 340).

We have only to ask how the sociologist is to produce his description of 'real-world events' or how he is to communicate 'seen but unnoticed background expectancies' to realise the absurdity of these prescriptions. Unless the sociologist is to be accorded the capacity, denied to ordinary mortals, to describe objects and events without the intervention of background expectancies or of tacit knowledge, then his accounts must be subject to precisely the same type of limitation as those of other observers. In that case his remarks cannot be 'taken on faith as an accurate portrayal of "what happened"' ([13] p. 6). For every socio-

11

logist's account we require a second account of how his background expectancies affected his account. This second account requires a third, and so on. The circularity of the prescribed procedure is obvious. We are faced with an infinite regression at no stage of which is it possible to escape the determination of seen but unnoticed background expectancies. These positions, therefore, lead to a complete relativism and to a necessary agnosticism with respect to the possibility of an objective knowledge of the world. The full significance of these authors' arguments should now be entirely clear. They may be directed against the objectivity of official statistics but they would dispose of the objectivity of all knowledge. What is at stake in these positions is not the utility of this or that lot of data, but the possibility of an objective knowledge of society. These remarks will be justified and elaborated in Chapter 2.

These opposed positions are united in the complicity of a common conception of knowledge as reducible to experience. If we are to construct an account of the production and possible use of statistical materials that does not fall into the relativistic or agnostic pitfalls of the ethnomethodologists, it is necessary to break completely with this conception of knowledge. Such a construction is attempted in Chapter 3, the first section of which is devoted to a commentary upon the faults and weaknesses of a particular set of official statistics, the Census of India, 1951. By way of this example, which is of course by no means unique, it is intended to show that, like all knowledge, official statistics must be analysed as a product. They are never mere givens to be taken as they are or else dismissed as inadequate. Like all products they must be examined in terms of the conditions and instruments of their production.[3] In the case of statistics we may distinguish between two sets of instruments – the 'technical' instruments of the social survey and 'conceptual' instruments, the system of concepts and categories governing the assignment of cases into classes. With these concepts (i.e. of 'technical' and 'conceptual' instruments), it is possible to demonstrate that the evaluation of statistical materials, their areas of ambiguity and indistinctness, of conceptual indeterminacy, requires no reference to the subjective experiences of officials and observers or to their

[3] See Bibliography for references on this conception of epistemology and the history of the sciences.

12

alleged 'meanings', 'tacit knowledge' or 'background expectancies'. It is also shown that, while the use of any given set of
statistics may pose its own specific theoretical problems, there are
no general theoretical problems involved in the use of official
statistics as such.

2. SOME ARGUMENTS CONCERNING THE PRODUCTION AND USE OF OFFICIAL STATISTICS

CHAPTER 1 has identified two types of argument relating to the production of official statistics and their use by social scientists: that concerned with the making and recording of observations and that concerned with the processing and assembling of statistical materials out of observers' reports. These appear to show that official statistics do not and cannot correspond to the structure of 'real-world' objects and events and that they cannot be taken as a more or less reliable account of some real situation. Following a short exposition, I shall argue that these positions must lead to an agnosticism with respect to what Douglas calls 'real-world' objects and to a complete and systematic relativism. These consequences are a necessary effect of their authors' 'positivist' conception of knowledge as founded upon individual experience together with their effective denial of a pre-theoretical observation language by the sociologising of the categories of observation and description.

First, consider the question of observation. Any observer, whether he be a probation officer, census enumerator, sociologist, or whatever, proceeds by making reports on the events, situations, or objects which he has observed. In writing up his report he uses certain features of the observed event to assign the event itself, or certain individual participants thereof, into what appear to be the appropriate categories. In the case of suicide statistics, for example, the coroner or some other official has to decide whether a given corpse is indeed dead and whether it is to be counted as a suicide. He makes his decision on the basis of certain investigations. Or again, a police officer has to decide whether a certain incident falls within the definition of a crime, which of several possible categories of crime it is to be recorded under, to which of many possible individuals it is to be attributed, and so on.

The social scientist or other researcher, who wishes to make use of these reports, is dependent upon the observer for his data. The difficulty with this appears to be

> that one is still relying upon human judgement for the data, not simply upon sensory experience, which one used [in the case of temperature measurement] to observe the mercury expansion and contraction against a calibrated scale, but actually upon the complex faculties of human judgements in interaction with each other.[1] ([14] p. 170).

How are these assignments of cases into categories produced? Douglas doubts whether suicide statistics are really aggregated measures of the same phenomena since the meaning of the term 'suicide' for the various officials who classify and tabulate deaths may not correspond to any one formal definition. For this reason it is necessary to consider both 'the objective criteria used to decide how to classify a death and the search procedures used in determining whether these criteria are met' ([14] p. 183). It is clear that two men may agree on the formal definition of suicide, yet disagree about the classification of a particular case. Douglas cites the example of a coroner for whom a death is classified as a suicide only if a suicide note is actually found with the body :

> The imputation of the official category of the 'cause of death' is very likely the outcome of a complex interaction process involving the physical scene, the sequence of events, the significant others of the deceased, various officials, the public, and the official who must impute the category ([14] p. 190).

Cicourel maintains that the organisational decisions of law-enforcement personnel (or, indeed, of anyone else) must be understood in terms of their stock of knowledge about the social

[1] Douglas' assertion, in the discussion of this point, of a continuity between sensory experience of warmth and the scientific measurement of temperature is, of course, entirely mistaken. See Bibliography and also the example given in the Appendix of the measurement of time.

types they encounter in the course of their work : that is, in terms of the background expectancies which govern all social interaction. Background expectancies are defined, following Garfinkel, as a scheme of interpretation used by members of society in rendering appearances recognisable and intelligible (i.e. as familiar events or events of a familiar type). Background expectancies

are sanctioned properties of common discourse. They furnish a background of seen but unnoticed features of common discourse whereby actual utterances are recognised as events of common, reasonable, understandable, plain talk[2] ([13] p. 8).

It follows that 'what members and researchers label "data" and "findings" can only be understood by reference to the background expectancies' ([13] p. 8). These background expectancies function in making an environment of objects recognisable and intelligible to the observer himself and, through his reports, to other individuals. The probation officer, for example, has to transform his conversations with and observations of his 'clients' into written reports which can be taken as an accurate account of the reported events. Cicourel's book

directs the researcher's attention to the theories of delinquency employed by laymen and particularly to theories employed by the police, probation, and court officials when deciding the existence of delinquency . . . What is needed are studies showing how folk theories articulate with actual practice, adequate descriptions of the environment of objects attended by members, and the organising features of their practical activities ([13] p. 24).

Here the environment of objects after it has been transformed and rendered intelligible by background expectancies is to be compared with the untransformed (unintelligible?) environment itself, so that the effect of the background expectancies may be assessed.

[2] Cicourel's discussion of this point follows Garfinkel's paper 'Studies of the Routine Grounds of Everyday Activities', [20] pp. 35–75. The quotation is taken from p. 41.

The compilation of social statistics involves the collation of reports from numerous observers, each with his own background expectancies and commonsense theories regarding the phenomena to be recorded. As a result of differences in these background expectancies we should expect to find that apparently identical cases are sometimes recorded differently by different observers and that identical records are sometimes the result of quite different phenomena. It follows that any set of statistics in which many observers' reports are aggregated cannot reasonably be taken to represent the incidence of the same phenomena. They cannot, therefore, be interpreted without reference to the background expectancies of the observers on whose reports the statistics are based. In addition, it should be noted that the accounts given in the initial reports are themselves subject to progressive transformations so that, for example, they can be 'viewed as falling under legal rules'. In the case of legal proceedings

> . . . each successive stage of legal decision-making transforms the object or event so that the contingencies, the situation in which the actor interprets what is going on, the kind of 'theorising' or thinking employed are progressively altered, eliminated, and reified, as the case proceeds up the legal machinery and reaches the stage of a hearing, trial, or appellate jurisdiction ([13] p. 50 and p. 53).

Much of Cicourel's text is devoted to the analysis of these processes of transformation. At each stage in the processing of a case it is the background expectancies of, and the relationships between, each of the participants that determines how the case is to be categorised as the outcome of that stage. Apart from this negotiation of 'what happened' we must also consider the routine collation and coding of case reports. Here it frequently happens that the case report itself is insufficient to determine the category that the case should fall under. Cicourel gives an example of the difficulties involved in coding from his own research :

> Many impasses occurred, and these were finally resolved by the head research assistant more or less by fiat in order to settle the

matter and so that they could all get on with the work ([13] p. 106).

Cicourel does not appear to be concerned with the significance or the extent of this classification by fiat in relation to the final tabulation. With respect to which categories do these difficulties arise? What proportion of cases must be decided in this fashion: 0·01 per cent, 5·0 per cent, 95 per cent? If it is the last, then the final tabulation is obviously worthless; if the first, then classification by fiat may be ignored as a source of error in the tabulation in question. It is clear that the identification or problematic categories and of the proportion of problematic cases is a necessary first step in any modification of coding procedures intended to reduce the significance of classification by fiat. Cicourel fails to examine these questions. It would seem that he has no interest in the identification and, therefore, the control of possible sources of error. Douglas' examination of the production of suicide statistics betrays the same lack of interest in the quantitative effect of various sources of error. He is content to show that such sources exist[3] ([14] p. 209 ff.). Both authors are concerned to demonstrate the necessity of classification by fiat, of 'reification', the necessary 'freezing' of accounts, and the like. More precisely, their demonstration concerns the necessary inadequacy or incompleteness of any set of categories and instructions with respect to the phenomena in question. 'The meanings of perceptual phenomena presented to the observer are always uncertain to some degree' ([14] p. 184).

The reader will have noticed that a crucial role is played in these arguments by a more or less explicit opposition between 'theoretical' and 'observational' categories. The latter relate to the structure of 'real-world' objects and events, while the former designate the 'objects' or 'events' constructed in common-sense or in scientific discourse out of these 'real-world' events through the operation of background expectancies, tacit knowledge, and the like. I have already cited Douglas' injuction concerning 'the dangers involved in constructing theories without a firm foundation

---

[3] For Douglas the effect of what he supposes to be the distribution of attempted concealment is to 'produce a fundamental bias in the testing of almost all sociological theories tested with official statistics, a bias that would result in the acceptance of most of these theories regardless of the state of real-world events'. (p. 216)

of careful descriptions of real-world events' ([14] p. 340). The same author denies the existence of real suicide rates:

> The term 'potential suicide rate' is used here rather than the more normal term 'real suicide rate', simply because it is a fundamental part of the argument throughout this work that there does not exist such a thing as a 'real suicide rate'. Suicides are not something of a set nature waiting to be correctly or incorrectly categorised by officials. The very nature of the 'thing' is itself problematic so that 'suicides' cannot correctly be said to exist (i.e., to be 'things') until a categorisation has been made[4] [14] p. 196 note).

It seems that we are concerned with two different orders of things. On the one hand there are real-world things or events – real or proper things. On the other hand there are things that are not things at all – things improper. The latter are the result of the imposition of an order or classification of things proper by some observer. Thus, what is called the real suicide rate is the product of further transformations and codifications of numerous things improper by some bureaucratic apparatus. The real suicide rate is a function of the organisation producing suicide statistics.[5]

Cicourel, as we have seen, treats background expectancies as transforming and rendering intelligible a given environment of objects. The sociologist is urged, amongst other things, to examine the functioning of these background expectancies by examining the transformed product in relation to the given objects. In an earlier book we find a similar distinction in his opposition between literal measurement and measurement by fiat:

[4] It is characteristic of the astonishing lack of rigour of this text that, within the space of a few pages, suicides can appear both as things improper (the product of classification) and as things proper, existing independently of any attempt at classification. 'I am arguing that the probabalistic nature of the categorisations is sufficient in itself to account for the regularity of suicide statistics in any given society, or, at least, most of the regularity. But if the suicide deaths [i.e. before categorisation] are themselves probabalistic, so that we get a two-stage probabalistic process, then we can expect even greater regularity than would otherwise have been the case.' (p. 200 note)

[5] See the following on 'real' rates: '. . . culturally defined real amount of crime for police, and culturally defined real demand for clinic services for clinic personnel – "exist" but only in the peculiar sense in which cultural objects, sociologically speaking, are said to "exist": their existence consists only and entirely of the likelihood that socially organised measures for the detection and control of deviance can be enforced.' ([20] p. 215 note)

19

Literal measurement refers to an exact correspondence between the substantive elements and relations under study and the ordered elements and relations of the measurement system. Measurement by fiat is an arbitrary or forced correspondence between elements, relations and operations ([12] pp. 225–6).

It is now necessary to examine the place and function of this apparent distinction between 'theoretical' and 'observational' categories in the discourse of Cicourel, Douglas and their associates. In particular I shall be concerned with the disastrous theoretical effects of these authors' combination of a positivist conception of knowledge with their failure to maintain a rigorous distinction between these two sets of categories. Distinctions of this type have been developed and elaborated in contemporary empiricist philosophy of science, especially in those variants loosely referred to as logical empiricism and logical positivism (see Appendix). They also appear in a more or less vulgarised form in the sections on science, theory and the like in textbooks on research methods.

At first sight it seems that, over and above any consideration of bias, error and reliability, the arguments presented above against the use of official statistics as data by sociologists are directed against the absence of any clear correspondence rules for the categories appearing in official tabulations. That is, there is no clear or unambiguous interpretation of these official categories in terms of some well-defined set of 'real-world' objects or events. There appear to be two reasons for this absence of correspondence rules. First, we have no reason to expect that the meanings of the given official categories are the same for different observers or that they share the same background expectancies. That is, the observers cannot be expected to follow the same rules in assigning cases to the given categories. It follows that the mere aggregation of different observers' reports must produce a meaningless jumble of figures. Secondly, the production of statistics from observers' reports is not normally reducible to the simple aggregation of given category assignments. Rather, as we have seen, the observer's report itself is the basis of a process of negotiation and argument. In the course of this process, the observer's comments are interpreted and used as grounds for the assignment of the case to its appropriate category. This assignment is the result of an act of judgement and necessarily involves a certain arbitrary element. Since 'social meanings are fundamentally problematic both for the members of the society and for the scientists attempting to observe, describe and explain their actions' ([14] p. 339), all classification is, to a greater or lesser extent, classification by fiat. While this classification is guided by certain rules, it can never be completely determined by them.

It follows that there is, at best, only a tenuous connection between some set of statistics and the 'real-world' objects or events to which they are intended to refer. In particular, then, the sociologist or other interpreter cannot legitimately assign correspondence rules to statistical categories by way of what Douglas calls a 'formal definition'. That is, he cannot assume a uniform interpretation of these categories in terms of observable objects and events. Such interpretation would be legitimate only if it could be demonstrated that the initial observers and the compilers of the statistics in question used the same rules of categorisation, and that these rules were sufficient to eliminate classification by fiat in every case.

It would seem that what is at stake in these arguments is the failure of the tabulations given in official statistics to correspond to observable differences and distinctions between 'real-world' objects. Such a position is certainly intrinsic to, for example, Douglas' attack on sociologists' use of official statistics on suicide and his call for the construction of theories with 'a firm foundation of careful descriptions of real-world events. The immediate task before us must clearly be that of providing such careful, comparative descriptions of many forms of social action' ([14] p. 340). Here 'careful, comparative description' of 'real-world events' is clearly presumed to be possible. Unfortunately it is not, and cannot be, provided by official statistics. Again, Cicourel, as we have seen, writes of background expectancies as schemes of interpretation, whereby members of a society organise and transform an environment of objects to produce statistics or other facts to be labelled data. Sociologists cannot assume that the structure of such 'data' corresponds to the structure of the given environment of objects.

What is needed are studies showing how folk theories articulate with actual practice, adequate descriptions of the environment of objects attended by members, and the organising features of their practical activities. How natives describe events and objects provides a basis for contrasting abstract notions such as 'contract', 'debt', 'crimes', and 'rape' with folk or members' categories[6] ([13] p. 24).

This, too, suggests that the environment of objects and members' background expectancies can be observed and described. Official statistics, since they are produced by and through these background expectancies, can never provide reliable descriptions of the environment of objects.

In these arguments official statistics are contrasted unfavourably to accurate descriptions of real-world events. The latter are presumed to be attainable, at least in principle, and to involve a set of categories which are not merely '*assumed* to be the only right categories for understanding the social world' ([15] p. 265). Sociologists are attacked for using official statistics when they should be using these latter descriptions. Here observational categories function to establish the possibility of accurate descriptions of real phenomena, which provide the basis for the rejection of the use of official statistics. In addition, these accurate descriptions are to provide the basis for the development of theories and of theoretical categories with well-defined and unambiguous correspondence rules relating them to observational categories. Unfortunately, it turns out that the alleged observational categories are not independent of background expectancies and that the required accurate descriptions are unrealisable in principle.

Note first that the possibility of accurate descriptions of real-world events ensures that the difficulties relating to the production of official statistics can, in principle, be corrected or, at least, contained – by requiring observers to use observational rather than theoretical (i.e. common-sense or scientific) categories, and so on. This may be difficult to achieve in the short term, but it is easy to see that improvements in this direction could be made. In fact, however, we have seen that the texts of Cicourel and

[6] This requires that 'meanings' themselves be directly observable. McHugh ([31] p. 4) argues that 'the activity of defining a situation is an *observable* and hence methodologically necessary display of the various abstractions that generally pass for the workings of society'. In this case we need studies of how sociologists define the situations in which they study how people define situations.

Douglas do not show the slightest concern with the possible improvement or correction of crime or suicide statistics or with the estimation and control of possible sources of error.

In the light of the alleged need for accurate descriptions of 'real-world events', 'the environment of objects attended by members', and the like, this lack of concern for the corrigibility of existing descriptions must appear somewhat surprising. In fact, the apparent corrigibility of official statistics (in principle) is an illusion. This follows because the arguments used to dispose of official statistics must also dispose of the very possibility of accurate description. The apparent distinction between observational and theoretical categories must, therefore, collapse.

It is not difficult to see why this must be so. Cicourel has suggested that

> we can view religious dogma and science as both ideologies and bodies of knowledge, each with its own theoretical assumptions, methods, and rules for admitting propositions into its respective corpus of knowledge. The problems of knowledge, therefore, can be viewed from the perspective of the sociology of knowledge : the world of observables is not simply 'out there' to be described and measured with the measurement systems of modern science, but the course of historical events and the ideologies of a given era can influence what is 'out there' and how these objects and events are to be perceived, evaluated, described, and measured ([12] p. 38).

In his later work what is 'out there' for any given individual appears as the effect of the work of his background expectancies in transforming his environment of objects into intelligible phenomena. The sociologist in his examination of the 'knowledge' of this individual is enjoined to make visible the 'unstated and seen but unnoticed background expectancies' together with the environment of objects which they transform. This position necessarily induces an inescapable circularity in which the prescribed comparison of observer's report and environment of objects is invariably displaced into the comparison of one observer's report with another's.

Suppose, to take an example bearing on Cicourel's own work, we are concerned with the way in which the background expectancies of some police officer transform his experiences with juveniles into reports relating to juvenile crime and delinquency. We may proceed by observing his participation in various real-world events and examining the reports he makes of them. In this case we have two sets of reports: the policeman's reports and those of an observer of the events related in the first set of reports. Before these latter reports can be used to estimate the effects of background expectancies in producing the former, we need to know how our observer's descriptions relate to the environment of objects in question. To achieve this we call in a third observer to examine our observer of the police officer. This leads to the absurdity of an infinite regression, at no stage of which is the environment of objects available other than in the form of an observer's report (rendered intelligible by the action of his background expectancies).

A similar inaccessibility of real-world events to objective inspection appears in Douglas' writings as a result of what he terms the 'essentially problematic nature' of social meanings. Thus, he deplores the failure of sociologists 'to see that an *official* categorisation of the cause of death is as much the end result of an *argument* as such a categorisation by any other member of society' ([14] p. 229). Since any categorisation, even the sociologist's, is the result of human judgement and argument, we can never do more than compare one judgement with another and neither to the 'real-world events' to which they refer.[7]

In both cases, then, we have the following position. There is an environment of objects and real-world events with respect to which official statistics must be judged totally inadequate. These objects and events are never available to scientific scrutiny except in the form of observers' reports – including those of the scientist himself.[8] These reports are always already organised by background expectancies, observers' common-sense theories, tacit knowledge, and so on.

It follows that there exists a realm of objects that can never

[7] Notice that a sociology of knowledge which sees knowledge as an effect of assumptions, 'background expectancies', 'tacit knowledge', must preclude the identification of 'real-world events' with intersubjective validity. Thus, while Carnap [10] can assume the existence of a pre-theoretical observation language, such an assumption must be problematised by a sociology of knowledge.

[8] These objects and events correspond to Schutz' realm of directly experienced social reality (see [23]).

be known – Cicourel's environment of objects, Douglas' real-world events. That conclusion appears to be the import of the following :

> Science and scientific method as means of viewing and obtaining knowledge about the world around us provide those who accept its tenets with a grammar that is not merely a reproducing instrument for describing what the world is all about, but also shapes our ideas of what the world is like, often to the exclusion of other ways of looking at the world. Language, then, and the cultural meanings it signifies, distorts and obliterates, acts as a filter or grid for what will pass as knowledge in a given era ([12] p. 35).

If 'language' or the 'grammar' provided by science or by religious dogma distorts, obliterates and filters, there must presumably be something that is distorted. This, whatever it might be, can never be known in an undistorted form. It follows that the forms and effectivity of the distorting mechanisms must be equally unknowable.

Thus, our authors' sociology of knowledge, their search for background expectancies, tacit knowledge, and so on, necessarily induces what seems to be a Kantian agnosticism with respect to our knowledge of 'real-world' objects and events. However, if we are to appreciate the full depths of the irrationalism of this conception, we must recognise that the 'background expectancies' and 'tacit knowledge', which render intelligible the environment of 'things-in-themselves', are not universal or necessary categories to thought. On the contrary, they vary from culture to culture, community to community and even from person to person. It is precisely this variation that is supposed to necessitate the sociology of knowledge in this conception.

The contrast between the Kantian agnosticism and that of the present conception may be expressed as follows. The universality of the Kantian categories serves to determine the limits of reason since all knowledge is produced in and by means of the categorical forms. These limits determine a realm within which rational forms of proof and demonstration are possible and necessary – the rational forms are governed by the universal categories. Thus, the Kantian conception attempts to ensure the possibility of rational

25

knowledge within certain limits.[9] The effect of the sociologising of the categories in terms of non-universal background expectancies and tacit knowledge is precisely to eliminate the universal foundation of rational forms of proof and demonstration. What appears to be 'rational' does so only as an effect of background expectancies. With different expectancies this appearance of 'rationality' will vanish. In this conception there are no limits to reason, beyond which it may not operate and within which it may. There is no reason, merely a multiplicity of individual 'reasons', each with its own unknown and unknowable forms of distortion and obliteration.

It should now be clear that the arguments of social phenomenology and ethnomethodology concerning official statistics lead inexorably to the denial of the possibility of rational knowledge, that this denial cannot be restricted to a limited domain of the materials used by sociologists, and that it must apply in full generality to all forms of rational knowledge.

What, then, must we make of these authors' accounts of the workings of statistics-producing organisations? These accounts are produced within an irrationalist problematic in which there is no place for rational proof and demonstration. It follows that the supposed demonstrations offered by these authors are theoretically worthless. A manuscript produced by a monkey at a typewriter would be no less valuable.

If this judgement seems harsh, consider what would be required to avoid it. What, in terms of their own epistemology, are the conditions in which the proofs and demonstrations offered by Cicourel and Douglas are, in fact, proofs and demonstrations and not a meaningless accumulation of marks on paper? These conditions are that the alleged limits of knowledge do not affect certain types of proof and of observation, namely, those used by our authors. To demonstrate that these conditions were indeed satisfied would require that the limits be known and that it is

[9] For Kant, 'our reason sees, so to speak, around it a space for knowledge of things in themselves, although it can never have determined concepts of them and is limited merely to experience'. *Prolegomena to Any Future Metaphysics* (Manchester: Manchester University Press, 1953) p. 119. I make no attempt to examine the coherence of the Kantian conception here. As Engels has pointed out: 'What is decisive in the refutation of this view has already been said by Hegel, insofar as this was possible from an idealist standpoint'. K. Marx and F. Engels, *Selected Works* one-volume edition (London: Lawrence & Wishart, 1969) p. 605. For a brief statement see, for example, paragraph 60 of Hegel's Encyclopaedia, in Wallace (ed.), *The Logic of Hegel* (London: O.U.P., 1968) pp. 114–20.

possible to go beyond them – precisely to show that they do not apply in the case in question. This requirement contradicts the very principles on which these authors base their demonstrations.

It might be suggested that, as I have pointed out, numerous passages in these authors' texts appear to present a much weaker version of their thesis: namely, that 'careful descriptions of real-world events' are, in fact, possible, but that official statistics do not provide them. Official statistics would then be corrigible in principle. Such a 'weak' thesis is entirely incompatible with the epistemological position adopted by these authors, and amounts, in effect, to the assertion that the influence of background expectancies on observation can be controlled and even overcome if suitable precautions are taken. A perfectly consistent positivist critique of official statistics could, indeed, be developed along these lines, but it is not developed by Cicourel or Douglas. Such a critique would attempt to demonstrate that the gross error, that is, the deviation from the 'true' distribution, in some types of statistics, was so great as to render them virtually useless. The limitations of this conception of error are discussed in Chapter 3.

3. THE RATIONAL EVALUATION OF OFFICIAL STATISTICS

IN contrast to the position examined in Chapter 2, the more orthodox texts on social statistics assume that, in principle, a true allocation of individuals into response categories is obtainable. Any given statistical distribution is to be evaluated with respect to its deviation from the presumed true distribution, that is, with respect to its net or gross response error. Survey methodology aims to obtain the minimum possible error within the limits set by time and available resources. The presumed true distribution is assumed to be independent of any investigation. I shall argue that such a conception of error is unacceptable as far as empirically given populations are concerned and that, in fact, the plausibility of this conception depends on ignoring the theoretical character of survey or census categories and of the instructions which determine how individual cases are to be assigned to them. These points are argued with the help of an extended example dealing with agrarian statistics.

The positivist conception of social statistics denegates the place and function of theory in their production. The anti-positivist positions examined above do likewise. Where one locates the source of deviation from the real in errors of observation and recording, errors that are avoidable in principle and can be minimised in practice, the other locates this deviation in the necessary structures of human experience. What is corrigible in the first case is necessarily incorrigible in the second. The common error in these positions lies in their attempts to establish human experience as the foundation of knowledge and in their consequent denegation of the place of concepts and of rationalist forms of demonstration. By examining social statistics with reference to the instruments of their production I shall argue that, contrary to the positions examined in Chapter 2, the evaluation of official, or other, statistics requires no reference to the 'subjective experience' of enumerators or officials.

(i) Agrarian Categories in the Census of India, 1951[1]

In the 1951 Census of India enumerators were asked to distribute persons engaged in agriculture into four classes in accordance with the following instructions :

> Write 1 for a person who cultivates land owned by him; 2 for a person who cultivates land owned by another person; 3 for a person who is employed as a labourer by another person who cultivates land; 4 for a person who receives rent in cash or kind in respect of land which is cultivated by another person. (Tables, p. ix)

Of the 249 million persons classified as depending on agriculture for their livelihood, 'rent receivers' or 'non-cultivating owners' and their dependents accounted for 5·3 millions. The class of 'owner-cultivators' amounted to 167·3 million, roughly two-thirds of the agricultural population. 'Tenant-cultivators', on the other hand, form a much smaller class, only 31·6 million or 13 per cent of the agricultural population. In contrast to the total figure for all cultivators (198·9 million), the number of cultivating labourers and their dependents is a mere 44·8 million, 18 per cent of the agricultural population. The proportion of cultivators to cultivating labourers shows that the number of cultivators who are also employers of labourers (in addition to, or in place of, labour performed by themselves or their family) must be relatively small. The Census Report states that 'the preponderance of "owner-cultivators" is the most important and characteristic feature of our agricultural class structure' (Report, p. 96). Compared with the previous tabulated census figures (for 1931), these results indicate a significant increase in the proportion of cultivators together with a corresponding decline in the proportion of labourers, and an absolute decline in the number of tenants.

[1] Much of the exposition in this section relies on the analyses in Thorner [37]. The third part of that text contains a valuable critical examination of the methods used in censuses and sample surveys on the agrarian situation in India. References to the Census Report are taken largely from vol. I, part IA (referred to as Report) and vol. I. part IIB (referred to as Tables). The West Bengal and Madhya Pradesh Reports appear in vols. VI and VII respectively.

The widespread demands for land reform at that time and since suggest either that a significant proportion of the agrarian population have an erroneous conception of the system of land tenure or else that the census results themselves are misleading. Let us examine this second possibility and consider how the distribution of the agricultural population into classes was arrived at. According to the instructions quoted above, it is clear that two distinctions are of crucial importance : between those who cultivate (classes 1 and 2 in the above instructions) and those who do not (classes 3 and 4, i.e. cultivating labourers and rent-receivers) and between owners and non-owners of cultivated land. In the first case we must distinguish cultivation of the land from 'performance of the labour necessary for cultivating the land' (Tables, p. xii). The cultivating labourer is

an employee of a cultivator, whose business merely is to perform physical labour in the manner required by the cultivator. The cultivator is the manager of cultivation – he is the person who decides how and when or where the various operations of cultivation should be undertaken, and who sees to it that they are properly undertaken. He is the person who accepts the risks of cultivation. The nature of the income obtained by these cultivators is quite different from that of the cultivating labourer. The cultivator gets the net profits of cultivation, i.e., what remains of the produce of the land after expenses are met. The cultivating labourer gets agricultural wages. The livelihood of the cultivating labourer is part of the expenses of cultivation[2] (Report, pp. 94–5).

Cultivation, in effect, amounts to the exercise of decision. It may also involve the performance of the labour necessary for the cultivation of the land, but it need not do so. The cultivator runs the risks of cultivation and receives his income in the form of profits on his stock or capital. We will return in a moment to the significance of the categories of 'wages', 'profits', 'decision-making', 'risks', 'employer' and 'employee' in respect of Indian Agriculture. Before doing so it is necessary to distinguish between

[2] These criteria are used in the British Census to distinguish socio-economic groups 13 (farmers – employers and managers) and 14 (farmers – own account) from 15 (agricultural workers).

the two sub-groups of cultivators : the owner-cultivators and the tenant-cultivators.

The term 'owned', used in relation to land, includes every tenure which involves the right of permanent occupancy of land for purposes of cultivation. Such right should be heritable; it may be, but need not necessarily be also transferable. (Report, p. 95)

An owner, in this sense, may be unable to sell his land or to use it for non-agricultural purposes. He may be obliged to pay rent to a landlord who, for census purposes, is disqualified from the title of 'owner' because his legal rights are 'strictly limited to the receipt of a rent' (Report, p. 93). The tenant-cultivator is then defined as any cultivator who is not an owner. This category, therefore, includes cultivators who are employees of owners (i.e. farm managers) together with sub-tenants, tenants-at-will and other holders of weak or short-term tenancies.

The reader will have little difficulty in recognising in the rent-receiver, cultivator and cultivating labourer the representatives of the three great classes of classical political economy : the owners of land, capital and labour-power respectively. Rent, the income of the landowner, 'is that portion of the produce of the earth, which is paid to the landlord for the use of the original and indestructible powers of the soil'. The labourer receives wages and the 'remaining quantity of the produce of the land, after the landlord and labourer are paid, necessarily belongs to the farmer, and constitutes the profits of his stock'.[3] Yet the census definition of ownership cuts across these categories. The landowner of Smith and Ricardo is precisely the rent-receiver (i.e. non-owner) in the census schema, whilst the capitalist tenant farmer of the classics appears in the census as the owner-cultivator. There is no place in Ricardo's schema corresponding to the category of tenant-cultivator (except, of course, for the farm manager).

Unfortunately for the Census Commissioner, the classical trinity formula hardly corresponds to the system of agricultural production in India. In particular, there is no numerically signi-

[3] David Ricardo, *On the Principles of Political Economy and Taxation* (Harmondsworth: Penguin Books, 1971) p. 91 and p. 132. A further portion of the produce goes towards replacing constant capital used up in the course of production. This portion is systematically ignored in the texts of classical political economy.

ficant class in the Indian agrarian scene that can be equated to Smith and Ricardo's capitalist tenants who lease land from landlords, invest their own stock, and direct their hired labourers in producing crops for the sake of earning a net profit.

How does the use of what Thorner calls 'these alien concepts' ([37] p. 139) affect the distribution of the agrarian population into census classes? Class 1 (owner-cultivators) includes proprietors, tenants of the State and a whole range of tenants of landlords provided that they can be classified as taking the 'risks of cultivation' and the managerial decisions as to when and where to plant, and provided that they hold their tenancy on a permanent or semi-permanent basis. This category includes capitalist farmers who employ labourers and produce a commercial crop for the market and a vast mass of peasant producers with a variety of relatively secure rights to the land who may be more or less integrated into the market economy. Class 2, as we have seen, throws together the least secure peasant producers and the managers of commercial agricultural enterprises.

In addition to this lumping together of radically heterogeneous elements into each of the four classes, the criteria laid down for the allocation of individuals into classes allowed for a measure of self-selection by members of the target population and imposed a considerable burden of choice on the enumerators. It is clear, for example, that the category of cultivator may include the zamindar or proprietor, who retains part of his estate as a home farm for which he makes the responsible decisions. These decisions may range from the allocation of land and seed to cropsharers (who may represent themselves as tenant cultivators) to the day to day management of a capitalist farm. The hereditary tenant or leaseholder of a parcel of the same proprietor's land may represent himself as an owner-cultivator while his sub-tenant appears as a tenant-cultivator (i.e. as a person who cultivates land 'owned' by another person). Those who labour for the above cultivators are cultivating labourers – unless, that is, they are members of a cultivator's family or are themselves cultivators of some other parcel of land. With such definitions the category of cultivator may include a zamindar who does no farming himself, but lets a portion of his land to share-croppers, a capitalist farmer employing wage-labour, and even some of the employees of this farmer.

32

What happens to individuals who appear to fall under more than one of the agrarian categories? The enumerators' instructions provide that where a person has several sources of income the one which provides the largest portion of the whole is to be recorded as his principal means of livelihood. Individuals are classified according to their principal means. This raises two major problems for the enumerator. First is the difficulty of comparing different portions of the total annual income where part of this 'total income' is in money and other parts are in the form of various agricultural or manufactured products or in services rendered in exchange for labour or produce. Where a substantial portion of the income does not take the form of money or of other commodities, there is no uniform standard with which the relative contributions of the different forms of income can be compared.[4] Secondly, because the enumerator must base his classification on the answers to a few simple questions, many individuals may effectively choose what is to be recorded as their principal means of livelihood. The State Superintendent for West Bengal notes that labourers 'who did a little share-cropping preferred to be recorded as share-croppers i.e. as tenant-cultivators) to being called agricultural labourers'. At the other extreme 'the scare of zamindari abolition and the hope that in the event of it maturing a proprietor would be allowed to cling to those plots which he could show as his own . . . drove many a proprietor to declare himself under livelihood 1 although his main income lay in the collection of rents' (West Bengal Report, pp. 347–51).

According to these same instructions, all persons in receipt of an income deemed sufficient for their own maintenance are classed as self-supporting and classified according to their principal means of livelihood. Others are classified as dependent and their principal means of livelihood is recorded as that of the head of the household. This classification into self-supporting and dependent involves a calculation that the majority of Indian families are in no position to make. In particular, the head of the household must be able to calculate the total income, the share of that income attributable to himself and the shares attributable to each of

---

[4] Certain authors, Thorner included, transform this feature into one of the essential characteristics of peasant economy. This is seen as a distinctive type of economy with the peasant family farm as its basic economy unit. This conception is discussed in the conclusion. The classical exposition is in Chayanov [11].

the other members, the amount necessary to sustain himself and the amounts necessary to sustain each of the other members of the household. Finally, he must compare the amounts required for sustenance in each case with the corresponding estimated income. In the absence of a common accounting unit (money) for each of the contributions to and outgoings from the family income, such calculations are almost impossible.[5]

These few indications are sufficient to show that the 1951 Census does not give a reliable representation of the system of land tenure in Indian agriculture. The census instructions impose a considerable burden of choice upon the individual enumerator so that, in practice, there is no uniform set of criteria for the allocation of individuals into classes. Such a situation might, in terms of the positions discussed in Chapter 2, be described as one of 'classification by fiat'. The Census Report must, as we have seen, considerably understate the proportions of rent-receivers and of cultivating labourers and it must inflate the proportion of owner-cultivators. Thorner goes so far as 'to wonder whether the agrarian categories of the 1951 Census were framed primarily for collecting economic statistics or for moulding public opinion against land reform' ([37] p. 143).

(ii) *Response Error and the System of Categories*
In the example of the classification of the agrarian population of India in the 1951 Census, I have concentrated on what appear to be two distinct types of difficulty : difficulties resulting in the erroneous classification of individual cases, that is, response errors and difficulties arising from the use of 'these alien concepts' ([37] p. 139) in determining the four major agrarian categories. In fact, as we shall see, these difficulties are not entirely independent.

In the analysis of social statistics response error is normally defined in terms of some presumed true allocation of individuals into response categories. A standard text by Moser and Kalton, for example, assumes that for each individual covered by the

[5] The Commissioner for Madhya Pradesh states that 'although the instructions were clear that no detailed inquiry was necessary about the income of individuals in such cases and the word of the head of household was to be taken for granted, the tragedy was that the innocent village folks and their heads of households had no "word" to offer on the subject to the Enumerator who had eventually to sit down with them and had actually to estimate the income of different members after prolonged discussions to ascertain whether a particular member was an "earning dependent" or a "self-supporting person" within the meaning of the Census definition and instructions'. (Madhya Pradesh Report, p. 417.)

survey in question there is a unique individual true value for each possible response. 'This value is quite independent of the survey, of the way the question is asked and by whom. If we ask the respondent how old he is, there is one unique correct answer . . .'[6] ([32] p. 378). There are of course many questions for which it would be difficult to define an individual true value. 'However', the authors add, 'this difficulty is beside the point here.' The researcher tries to ascertain the individual true value in each case. The difference between this value and the response obtained defines an individual response error. Gross and net response errors are defined in terms of the response distribution and the presumed true distribution.

I return below to the conditions in which such a conception of error is theoretically acceptable. For the present, notice that numerous technical and procedural devices are available for reducing the incidence of error so defined and for estimating the probable range of uncontrolled error. Many of the difficulties of the 1951 Census can be attributed to technical or organisational inadequacy with respect to the use of such devices. The Superintendent for West Bengal noted that

> unlike the sorting into non-agricultural livelihood divisions made by a centrally supervised staff, trained and drilled into a knowledge of making these distinctions, the responsibility of placing the population into the four main agricultural classes was relegated to the enumerator on the spot. (West Bengal Report, p. 348)

It is indisputable that an improvement in the classificatory practice of enumerators – that is, a reduction of response error – would have resulted from the use of appropriate technical and organisational devices : the proper training and supervision of the enumerators, the conduct of pilot surveys, and pre-tests of portions of the census schedule to discover difficulties likely to be encountered in classification. However, the effectivity of such technical devices is limited by the effects of the system of categories

[6] It is characteristic of such discussions that the example given is theoretically trivial. It is possible to specify a set of procedures by means of which the investigator may, in the vast majority of cases, determine a unique 'age' for each individual within known limits. It is against such a uniquely determined 'age' that questionnaire responses may be assessed. It should be clear that age has not always been trivial in this sense – nor is it yet for many populations.

which enumerators have to use. In fact, as our example will have demonstrated, it is the use of this system of categories that determines the types of ambiguity that appear in respect of the classification of individuals. That is, it determines and generates the particular types of difficulty faced by enumerators – which difficulties are specific to the set of categories in question. Different categories would generate different forms of ambiguity. In addition, the application of the given categories determines a certain necessary extent of this ambiguity, i.e. that it is not restricted to an insignificant minority of cases. In other words, it determines both the necessity and the extent of what Cicourel would call 'classification by fiat'. In the face of this necessity what can be the effect of improved training and supervision? At best, if the system of categories is retained, it can ensure a certain level and type of uniformity in the enumerators' practice. In that case the necessity of 'classification by fiat' appears at a level other than that of the field worker. It does not disappear.

I have observed that the Census Report understates the proportion of rent-receivers (class 4) and of cultivating labourers (class 3) and that it inflates the proportion of owner-cultivators (class 1). Strictly speaking it is necessary to reject these formulations since they require the existence of a unique and true assignment of each member of the population into one of the four given classes. It is only with respect to such presumed true assignments that the census results may under- or over-estimate proportions. In fact, there can be no true assignment of the Indian population into these given categories and, therefore, no correct distribution from which the census results can deviate.

This system of classes is derived from the trinity formula of classical political economy articulated upon the additional census distinction between owners and non-owners. Leaving aside this last complication, we have the attempt to discover the three great classes of Smith and Ricardo in the Indian countryside. This attempt founders upon a difficulty identified in Marx's discussion of the conditions for the development of the theory of rent by Anderson and Ricardo. In respect of the clearing of estates in England Marx concludes that

in short none of the conditions of production are accepted as they have traditionally existed but are historically *transformed* in such a way that under the circumstances they will provide the most profitable investment for capital. To that extent, therefore, *no landed property* exists; it gives capital – i.e., the farmer – full scope, since it is only concerned with monetary income. . . . English conditions are the only ones in which *modern landownership*, i.e., landownership which has been modified by capitalist production, has been adequately developed.

As for the attempt to apply Ricardo's categories to conditions in which the capitalist mode of production does not exist (e.g. by Rodbertus in Pomerania),

it is as if a guild-master wanted, lock, stock and barrel, to apply Adam Smith's laws – which presuppose free competition – to his guild economy.[7]

While the capitalist mode of production is by no means absent from Indian agriculture,[8] it does not yet occupy a dominant place in the system of agricultural production. The census categories treat as capitalist an agrarian system in which capitalist production relations play a subordinate role. An effect of this error is that the census categories are specified in commodity terms so that non-commodity elements in the agrarian system must be mis-recognised or ignored. Thus, the census categories do not distinguish commodity relations (i.e., production of goods for sale, wage labour, etc.) and, therefore, fail to differentiate between capitalist farming (commodity production, wage labour), petty commodity production, subsistence agriculture and the various transitional forms. The Census Report, then, can give no indication of the extent or forms of penetration of commodity relations in the countryside.[9] The additional census distinction be-

[7] Karl Marx, *Theories of Surplus Value, Part II* (Moscow: Progress Publishers, 1968) p. 238
[8] 'There are without doubt some genuine capitalist farmers – e.g. in parts of the Punjab, Western U.P., Berar, and here and there elsewhere. It is, however, poor procedure to devise a set of categories appropriate to only a tiny minority of India's agriculturalists and then to try to force the great majority into an inapposite framework' ([37] p. 139 n.)
[9] Thorner's own proposed classification is no better in this respect. See *The Agrarian Prospect in India* (Delhi: Delhi University Press, 1956). Here he proposes to distinguish three basic groups: *mazdoor, kisan, malik*. The first are agricultural workers who may sometimes own small plots of land. They may be paid in money

tween owner-cultivators and tenant-cultivators does constitute a break with the classical formula of the three great classes. Nevertheless, the tenant-cultivator is still assumed to be a *cultivator* in the census meaning of the term – that is, the concept is specified in terms of commodity relations. The tenant-cultivator is a capitalist farmer who lacks a crucial condition of existence of capitalist farming : relative security of tenure. In this respect the census adaptation of the classical schema constitutes a partial and extremely misleading recognition of the inappropriateness of the classical formula.

These points need not be developed here. What must be emphasised in the present context is that here we confront a problem that is in no way reducible to the technical or procedural devices for dealing with response error. The categories as defined are mutually exclusive and a variety of ad hoc procedures ensure that their coverage of the agrarian population is exhaustive. Nevertheless, there is no true distribution of the population into this set of classes. This problem concerns the theoretical, or at least the conceptual, character of the system of census categories. It should be clear that this problem is not peculiar to the 1951 Census of India. It arises in respect of the system of categories of any set of social statistics.[10]

To elaborate, in the present example the census categories, together with their corresponding instructions and elaborations, constitute what, with slight exaggeration, may be called a theory of the elements of the agrarian situation in India – a theory which can be shown to be seriously misconceived. The census figures are a product of this 'theory'. More precisely, the categories and their elaborations constitute an instrument for the

---

or in kind or they may receive a portion of the harvest. The main difference between the other categories is that the *kisan* always works his own land (as owner or tenant) and obtains the major part of his income from this work. The *malik* obtains the major part of his income from land which he does not work. His income may be in money or in kind, he may let the land to tenant-farmers or share-croppers or he may work it himself by means of hired labour. It is clear that commodity relations have no pertinence for such a classification.

[10] Precisely similar points may be made with respect to attempted applications of statistics in other sciences. Bernard's discussion of this question is excellent in many respects, *An Introduction to the Study of Experimental Medicine* (New York: Dover, 1957) pp. 129 ff. 'We must first accurately define the conditions of each phenomenon; this is true biological accuracy, and, without this preliminary study, all numerical data are inaccurate . . . .' (p. 136). What is at issue here is not whether statistics are useful (as Cohen appears to assume in his 1957 Foreword), but the theoretical conditions of their application in the science in question.

production of knowledge, in this case for the production of census figures. This instrument in conjunction with technical[11] survey instruments produces the census returns. Differences in the technical instruments employed may lead to somewhat different final results. At present we are not concerned with differences of this order. The first instrument, the elements of our 'theory', functions by providing the enumerator, for example, with a system of distinctions and differentiations that are pertinent to the allocation of individuals into census classes. His instructions determine the precise effectivity of these pertinences and their hierarchical order of functioning. For example, the classification of an individual as self-supporting, earning-dependent or dependent, determines the criteria on which his allocation to one of the four classes depends. The differences pertinent to the first decision determine what is pertinent to the second. These same elements determine the non-pertinence of certain differences confronting the enumerator in his attempts to produce correct classifications and the impertinence of others. In this last case we have an inadequate conceptual determination of the 'correct' classification : the instructions produce conflicting category assignments, there is incomplete specification, and so on – e.g. with respect to a wage-earning share-cropper who rents out his own 'owned' land to a sub-tenant. The concrete forms of this inadequacy, that is, the concrete problems faced by the enumerator, are the effect of the given set of categories. A different set of categories, i.e. a different conceptual instrument, would produce a different set of problematic cases.

Here the system of categories in conjunction with specific technical instruments determines a distribution of the population into classes. It also determines, for a given population, the specific levels and forms in which the 'correct' classification of cases is found to be inadequately specified, a lack of specification whose effects appear in a certain level of arbitrariness, of classification by fiat, and so on. But this arbitrariness is not, as the authors considered in Chapter 2 would suggest, an effect of the consciousness of the enumerator. It is a determination of a con-

[11] 'Technical' is used here to refer to survey instruments whose production is independent of the particular system of categories in use. This terminology ('conceptual' and 'technical') is not entirely satisfactory, since what are called 'technical' instruments are themselves the product of a conceptual practice of a certain kind.

ceptual instrument, the system of categories, and is specific to that instrument.

Two further points must be made with regard to the census 'theory' of the elements of the agrarian situation in India. First, to talk of a theory in this context is not to suggest that there must exist a coherent theoretical discourse in which the census categories are generated and from which they may be derived, i.e. that there is an explicit and well-defined theoretical basis for the selection of categories. Nor is it even to suggest that the categories, their elaborations and instructions specify a relatively coherent system of concepts. Such rational coherence is certainly possible, although it may be difficult to achieve in practice, and desirable, if results are to be of any use to anyone, but it is by no means necessary. Sample surveys and censuses may be conducted on the basis of categories generated in an ad hoc fashion. In such cases we may have a conceptual instrument with little rational coherence. Nevertheless, it remains a system of concepts with determinate relations of hierarchy and subordination between them.

The second point is raised by the treatment of the census categories as erroneous and inadequate, by Thorner's reference to 'these alien concepts'. Does this mean that there are categories that are not erroneous, not alien? Does it mean that we have only to select the *real* categories, categories that are not just 'assumed to be the only right categories for understanding the social world' ([15] p. 265) but which *really* correspond to *real* differences between *real*-world events and objects?[12] Armed with such real categories, the problems of conceptual indetermination of correct classification would not arise; we would be left with the purely technical problems of supervision and training, of the layout of schedules to minimise mistakes, and so on. We need only pose the question of how they might be discovered to see that such real categories are a figment of the empiricist imagination. If we were to send into the field a team of ideal observers, stripped of all concepts (to avoid the possible influence of alien categories), they would return with nothing to report and no vocabulary with which to report it. Any proposed set of categories can only be evaluated in terms of existing knowledge, knowledge that is always already a product of some means of production of knowledge. There is no evaluation of categories against the real in person.

[12] This play on the word *real* cannot be discussed here. See [2] pp. 34–40.

No ideal set of categories given in advance of any investigation. The achievement of categories with a minimum of conceptual indetermination is always a product of knowledge. It is not the condition of the possibility of knowledge. It is in this sense that we can agree with Thorner's remark that 'in these matters truth yields itself very slowly' ([37] p. 186).

We are now in a position to return to a question raised at the beginning of this section in connection with response error. This is normally defined with reference to some presumed correct and unique distribution of the target population into response categories. It was shown above that any distribution is the result of a determinate process of production of knowledge, a process characterised by the conjunction of what I have called conceptual and technical instruments. There is no census or sample survey distribution that is not the product of some such conjunction. There is no correct and unique distribution that exists independently of its means of production, no distribution that is independent, in particular, of the system of categories into which the population is to be distributed. While it may be possible to conceive of a technically optimal distribution, one that is independent of the particular technical instruments of its production, such a distribution remains the product of its conditions. That is, it contains its own specific level of indeterminacy and, to that extent, fails to provide a unique, correct assignment for each individual. The system of categories itself imposes an irreducible limit to the effect of purely technical or procedural improvements. In this respect the discussion of response error and inter-enumerator variance[13] in terms of some presumed true assignment for each individual in the target population, and, therefore, of a true distribution for that population as a whole, is both misleading and misconceived.

Under what conditions is the conception of error in terms of unique, true individual responses theoretically acceptable? It is clear that these conditions can only be those in which the conceptual indetermination specific to the given categories can be shown to vanish. Short of collapsing into the empiricist haven of 'real' or 'observational' categories corresponding to the real struc-

[13] Inter-enumerator variance refers to the distribution of differences in response obtained by different enumerators. In the absence of bias, the 'true' distribution appears as a limiting case in which this variance vanishes. This effectively reduces 'true' to intersubjectively valid.

ture of the real world, we can see that such conditions can be satisfied only by an ideal population, one that is specifically constructed to distribute perfectly into the given categories without overlap and without ambiguity. Only with respect to such a constructed population can error be defined in terms of the deviation of responses from individual true values.

Such populations are never given to the researcher outside of statistical theory. Elsewhere they may be constructed for training purposes or for the testing of technical devices with respect to the conceptual instrument in question – e.g. is the questionnaire sufficiently 'powerful' to render the necessary pertinent distinctions in an unambiguous fashion? It follows that the evaluation of censuses or other surveys based on empirically given populations (i.e. not constructed) can never be reduced to the identification or estimation of errors resulting from the technical inadequacy of the agency with respect to its tasks. These tasks are never wholly technical. The improvement of censuses or other surveys is never reducible to purely technical modification.[14]

[14] Precisely similar points may be made with respect to sample surveys. We need only consider the results obtainable by a sample study of Indian agriculture using the above census categories to see the importance of this point. The tendency to reduce survey methodology to technical questions (statistical hypotheses, estimation, so-called 'causal analysis') can only be deplored. In these cases also, the system of categories induces a certain necessary level and form of indeterminacy in the sample returns, while the imposition of non-pertinence on certain types of difference may serve to limit the extent of apparent error. If interpretation is purely technical, this may lead to erroneous, if not completely meaningless, 'hypotheses' being accepted. In addition, the use of sample surveys poses problems concerning the theoretical conditions of the use of statistical sampling theory with respect to empirically given populations. These problems cannot be discussed here.

4. CONCLUSION

CHAPTER 1 of this text examined certain arguments advanced by some sociologists in recent years concerning the production of official statistics and their use in sociology. It was argued that such force as these arguments may possess cannot be restricted to the case of statistical materials but that they must be directed also, and without exception, against all materials used as evidence and against all rational forms of proof and demonstration. In fact, they derive largely from a more general critique of theoretical abstraction in the social sciences advanced by contemporary forms of social phenomenology and ethnomethodology. The latter seek to establish human experience, preferably undistorted by background expectancies, tacit knowledge, and the like, as the foundation of knowledge as against concepts and rationalist forms of proof and demonstration. Where the preferred forms of undistorted experience are thought to be unavailable we are told that objectivity is a mirage. Thus Cicourel has been quoted as stating :

> In recognising that we can generate only different glosses of our experiences, the ethnomethodologists try to underscore the pitfalls of viewing indexical expressions as if they could be repaired and thus transformed into context-free objective statements.[1]

Contrary to their authors' claims, the texts examined in Chapter 2 are not concerned with the fundamental problems of sociology.

[1] At the B.S.A. Conference, 1971 – paper by Phillipson and Roche, typescript p. 32. These positions carry to an extreme a tendency that has a long history in the social sciences: in sociology, for example, positions deriving from the *Geisteswissenschaften* tradition (Weber is the classic point of union of this tradition with the empiricism of conventionalist positivism), from American pragmatism, Schutz's phenomenology, etc.

43

There is no problem for science concerning the use of official statistics in the sense intended by these authors. Where there are problems for social scientists with respect to official statistics, these are neither of the kind nor of the generality suggested in these texts, and there is nothing to be gained but confusion by discussing official statistics in their terms.

This is not to say, of course, that there are no points of any substance to be found in their texts. Douglas and Cicourel are undoubtedly correct in pointing out that many sociologists have been uncritical in their use of social statistics. In such cases little value can be attached to those proofs or demonstrations in which the given statistics play an essential part – i.e. if their function is not reducible to mere illustration. This point may be generalised to cover all materials appearing as evidence in the course of argument. Their use is uncritical if there is no attempt to demonstrate that the materials in question can fulfil the function assigned to them. In the case of social statistics such demonstration must involve the examination of what I have called the 'technical' and 'conceptual' instruments with which the proffered statistics were produced. However, the existence in many cases of negligence in this respect in no way supports the more general arguments of the ethnomethodologists.

Chapter 3 examined a specific set of official statistics : the Census of India, 1951. The commentary and subsequent discussion indicated the terms in which the rational theoretical assessment of statistical materials may be undertaken. It was shown, in particular, that such assessment does not require reference to any 'subjective experience' on the part of enumerators or officials (to their background expectancies, meanings, or whatever). Insofar as the consciousness of such individuals does intervene in the assignment of cases into categories, the space for, and the effect of, such intervention is determined by the structure of the system of categories and not by any structure of the 'consciousnesses' concerned.

Official statistics are produced by a conjunction of 'conceptual' and 'technical' instruments. It follows that the evaluation of such materials for scientific purposes must never be restricted to a concern with more or less deliberate misrepresentation or with the identification of technical errors and inadequacies. These problems are undoubtedly important but, as we have seen, they

44

are not the only sources of a lack of objectivity on the part of statistical materials. In addition to their consideration, the rational evaluation and utilisation of statistics for scientific purposes must take account of the conceptual means of their production, that is, of the system of categories together with the instructions and elaborations in which they are specified. This means that it must depend on the theoretical interests of the science concerned, since it is these that determine what is required of the statistics if they are to be of use. Clearly, then, there is little of any value to be said concerning the generality of official statistics or even, apart from purely technical questions, concerning the utility, in general, of any given set of statistics. The usefulness of such statistics is a function of the theoretical problematic in which they are to be used and on the use to which they are to be put within it.

This last point may be simply illustrated. Consider the Census statistics first from the point of view of a Marxist analysis of the agrarian situation in India. In this problematic the agrarian system must appear as a determinate combination of capitalist and of various pre-capitalist elements. In examining the development of capitalism in Indian agriculture, it would be necessary to identify the extent and forms of penetration of commodity relations into the countryside. To this end it would be necessary, for example, that farms be classified according to their scale as economic enterprises (the value of their *commercial* product), the employment of wage-labour, the use of machinery and of commercial fertilisers, and so on. For persons who 'cultivated' land, in the census sense, and also worked as labourers for others, it would be important to ascertain whether his rent was due in money or else in labour or produce, whether he was employed as a free wage-labourer or worked under other conditions (e.g. in lieu of rent, in return for access to water, the loan of seed, out of 'respect' for the landlord) and so on. Census and other statistics will be evaluated in these terms.[2] It is clear that the crucial distinctions for this problematic between commodity and non-commodity relations are not pertinent to the sections of the Census covering Indian agriculture. For this reason alone, even apart from the many glaring technical errors, the agrarian classification – cover-

[2] For the analysis of agrarian statistics in this problematic there is still little to compare with Lenin's studies cited in the Bibliography.

ing some 70 per cent of the population – is of little scientific value. It can give no indication of either the extent or the forms of penetration of commodity relations into the countryside. Since it fails to distinguish commodity and non-commodity relations and, in effect, treats all agricultural production as capitalist or petty-commodity production, it can only produce a gross misrepresentation of the agrarian situation in India.

A different problematic must generate a different evaluation. Consider, for example, a case in which the peasant family farm appears as the basis of a distinct type of economic system ([11] and [38]). Chayanov develops the concept of the peasant farm

as a family labor farm in which the family, as a result of its year's labor, receives a single labor income and weighs its efforts against the material results obtained. ([11] p. 41)

Members of the family unit work on the family farm, as agricultural wage-labourers, as share-croppers, or even in factories, according to circumstances – that is, according to the consumer demand of the family unit as a whole and the available outlets for the family's labour resources. The income which the family, as an economic unit, obtains from these various outlays arrives in the form of wages, money from the sale of produce or the renting out of land, its own produce, products obtained by barter, and so on. The totality of these receipts constitute the 'single labor income' of the family. There is no single accounting unit according to which these various receipts can be compared or by which the relative contributions of various labours can be assessed. In this respect the peasant family farm, according to Chayanov, differs from the capitalist farm as an economic unit. The latter does have an accounting unit, money, by means of which a rational calculation of the optimal use of resources (i.e. of its capital stock) is possible.

I am not here concerned to evaluate Chayanov's position. In the present context the important point to note is that peasant farms may be more or less involved in commodity relations according to circumstances:

Yet, the organisational shape of the basic cell, the peasant family labor farm, will remain the same, always changing in particular features and adapting to the circumstances surrounding in the national economy. ([11] pp. 42–3)

Here the concept of the peasant economy covers a whole range of pre-capitalist and transitional forms of agricultural production. How are agricultural statistics to be evaluated in this case? Obviously the first question to be answered concerns the presence or absence of the peasant family farm as a distinct type of economic unit. Census categories will be assessed according to whether they allow this question to be answered. The question of whether such farms, if present, are engaged in commodity relations will be of secondary importance. From this position, too, the agrarian categories of the 1951 Census must be severely criticised. But here the critique will take a different form from the one sketched above.

It should be clear from these examples that the evaluation of social statistics for scientific purposes is always and necessarily a theoretical exercise and, further, that different theoretical problematics must produce different and sometimes contradictory evaluations of any given set of statistics. The evaluation of social statistics is never reducible to a purely technical evaluation. It might be added that official statistics are rarely collected with the interests of science as their primary concern. It is necessary, therefore, to distinguish between the categories appearing in the initial recording schedules and those appearing in the published reports. Information that is available in the schedules may be lost in the further process of tabulation and classification. In such cases, once the relations between the two sets of categories are known, it may be possible to reconstruct, or at least to estimate, theoretically important distributions – even if the published figures are worthless, taken as they stand. Such points will be familiar to anyone who has attempted to make serious theoretical use of available statistics.

Perhaps some additional remarks are required concerning the 'weak' thesis apparently suggested by numerous passages in the texts examined in Chapter 2 : the thesis that 'careful descriptions of real-world events' are possible, but that official statistics do not provide them – official statistics would then be corrigible in principle if not always in practice. If this thesis is to be maintained, it requires that strictly non-theoretical 'observational' categories exist so that statistics could, in principle, be compiled on the basis of these categories. Where this appeared to be impracticable, the categories used in tabulations could be explicitly and unambiguously defined in terms of the basic observational categories. Two types of critique of official statistics might then be maintained. First, that the given categories had no unambiguous definition in observational terms. This would imply that cases that should be distinct might be classed together and that cases that should be classed together might be classed separately. In addition, it might be argued that statistics-producing agencies were technically inadequate so that a large gross error might appear even when the first type of critique did not apply. I have shown in Chapter 2 that while a consistent positivist critique of official statistics might be developed along these lines, it would be incompatible with the epistemological position elaborated by Cicourel and Douglas. Such a positivist critique of statistical categories would itself be strictly non-theoretical – that is, it would not depend upon any particular theory and would consist entirely in a comparison of the definitions used in practice and strictly 'observational' categories. In fact, there are no observational categories of this kind. I have, therefore, argued in Chapter 3 and in the immediately preceding paragraphs that the evaluation of official statistics must be a properly theoretical exercise.

Finally, there are variants of the above 'weak' thesis that might appear to be of particular relevance to the study of suicide. These would include among 'real-world events' those allegedly taking place in the consciousness of actors : so that, for example, suicide would be defined in part by reference to the motivation of the actor. In these positions some, perhaps all, human activities are to be classified in terms of the meaning of the action for the actor concerned.[3] It might perhaps be said, following Winch, that the connection between the observed action and its meaning is an internal, logical one. In that case, two actions which appear to be identical to an observer but which have different meanings for

[3] There are many such variants, for example, in the work of Winch, in Schutz, in symbolic interaction, as well as ethnomethodology and, of course, in Weber: 'Sociology is a science which attempts the interpretative understanding of social action . . .' and 'In "action' is included all human behaviour when and insofar as the acting individual attaches a subjective meaning to it', *The Theory of Social and Economic Organisation* (New York and London: The Free Press, 1964) p. 88. The present author has adopted a similar position in some of his earlier work, e.g. *The Decline of Working Class Politics* (London: MacGibbon & Kee, 1971).

their actors are in reality two different things. Douglas himself feels that

> it is not possible for individuals to construct just any meanings whatsoever for their actions, though individual creativity does extend the limits immensely and all cases include imponderable idiosyncrasies. ([15] p. 268)

Whatever comfort sociologists may derive from the existence of these limits the difficulty of classifying apparently identical actions remains immense. Obviously the classification of actions that appear identical but have different meanings into the same category would only serve to confuse matters. Douglas has taken this argument to its astonishing conclusion in the case of the category of death. How, he argues, can we possibly understand something so immensely complex as 'death' in any terms other than those of the actors involved? Thus :

> when some *ronin* of Japan or some Asian Buddhists perform actions which lead to what American or European doctors classify as death, we must recognise that this is a classification by Western doctors, not by the actors involved. Their linguistic expressions for such actions may be totally different from the ones Western observers use and certainly might mean totally different things to the actors and the significant observers of these actions within their own cultures. ([14] p. 182)

Sociologists who, no doubt because of their training and cultural background, would tend to follow Western doctors in these matters would also find it difficult to observe the meanings of actors that Western doctors would classify as dead. Indeed, even in the case of actors who give every indication of being alive, such observation poses severe difficulties. In general, it would seem that any classification of readily observable activities by some observer or observers according to apparently discriminating features but without reference to the meanings of these activities is most unlikely to correspond to a similar classification according to the meanings of the actors concerned. To any such set of social statistics, we might say, there corresponds a certain distribution of meanings which have generated the observed and classified

49

activities. This latter distribution cannot be inferred from the given statistics. Regularities in the given statistics are most unlikely to correspond to regularities in the distribution of meanings and are more likely than not to be entirely illusory.

The requirement that actions be classified according to their meaning for the actors reduces directly to the above 'weak', i.e., positivist, thesis if 'meanings' are thought to be observable. If not we have the following position. The social scientist is given certain observational materials – social statistics, questionnaire responses, and so on. In order to account for the given facts, he requires certain additional materials, namely, the meanings of the recorded actions for the actors concerned. These meanings, unfortunately, are not given. Nevertheless, they must form an essential part of the explanation of the given facts. The social scientist may get round this difficulty by constructing ideal types : that is, models consisting of objects both of the order of the given facts and of the order of the non-given meanings. The model then combines imaginary meanings and contents of consciousness with the observable effects these meanings are supposed to produce.[4] The social scientist proceeds by comparing the facts of some given situation with his ideal type or else he produces a new model to fit the facts in question. He thus obtains knowledge of the operation of his models. Otherwise he is limited to producing a catalogue of situations which appear to fit his various imaginary models reasonably well.

Is it necessary to add that the introduction of unobservables in this fashion avoids none of the errors of positivism and that it merely complicates what is already unacceptable?[5]

<hr />

[4] See the following: '. . . The observations which go to make up a distribution of, say, types of cities, responses to questionnaire items, or occupational prestige categories are only half the picture. The distribution merely represents the "outer" horizon for which operational procedures have been devised. Yet the "meaning" of the distribution relies upon the common-sense knowledge which includes the observer's typifications of the world. . . . and his formalisation of the actor's typification which is inextricably woven into his response'. ([12] p. 223)

[5] I have discussed a position of this type at some length elsewhere. [23].

APPENDIX: ON OBSERVATIONAL CATEGORIES

THE empiricist process of knowledge presents a process that is conceived as taking place in the confrontation of a given subject and a given object. The process itself concerns an operation of abstraction on the part of the subject. To know is to abstract from the object its essence. Within this conception the status of the subject (psychological or transcendental ego, transcendental intersubjectivity, and so on), and, correlatively, of the object may vary. These variations define different variants of empiricism ([2] pp. 34–40). In contemporary philosophy of science (logical positivism, logical empricism) the subject is an ordinary human subject and the most elementary and basic items of knowledge are his experiences. In an early work, for example, Carnap takes the basic elements of knowledge to be 'total momentary experiences' or 'cross-sections of consciousness' and attempts to demonstrate both that any scientific proposition is reducible to a series of elementary propositions referring only to these basic elements and also that a physical object language is methodologically equivalent to a 'total momentary experience' language as a foundation for empirical knowledge.[1] Such a conception of knowledge, as in some way reducible to experience (which may be described in a 'psychological' or an equivalent 'physicalistic' language), governs the account of science and scientific method given in the standard methodological texts in the social sciences. It is shared, at this level, by ethnomethodology and social phenomenology.

Scientific discourse refers to objects (electrons, electromagnetic fields, imperialism, the capitalist mode of production) that are not objects of immediate human experience and do not appear to be reducible to such objects. If experience is to be the basis of

---

[1] R. Carnap, *The Logical Structure of the World* (London: Routledge & Kegan Paul, 1967 (first German edition, 1938)).

knowledge, how can we be sure that such discourse has any meaning, i.e. that it is not metaphysical?[2] It is in terms of this question that the relation between theoretical and observational categories appears as a methodological problem of the highest importance for empiricist philosophy of science. Carnap's work constitutes, perhaps, the most rigorous attempt to deal with his problem. A brief examination of his elaboration of the distinction between theoretical and observational languages will be followed by an indication of the theoretical effects of abandoning the distinction in this form within the empiricist conception of knowledge. Finally, I comment on the inadequacy of even the most rigorous attempts to reduce scientific knowledge to human experience.

(i) *Theory and Observation in Empiricist Methodology*

In discussions on the methodology of science, Carnap observes, it is 'customary and useful to divide the language of science into two parts, the observation language and the theoretical language'[3] ([10] p. 38). The former contains terms which designate observable properties and relations of things and events while the latter 'contains terms which may refer to unobservable events, unobservable aspects or features of events, e.g. to micro-particles like electrons or atoms, to the electro-magnetic field or the gravitational field in physics, to drives and potentials of various kinds in psychology, etc.'. This theoretical language (L_T) consists of terms which cannot be given explicit definitions on the basis of statements in the observation langugate (L_O). The absence of observable referents for theoretical terms raises the question of the criteria for the significance of L_T. This question concerns the

exact conditions which terms and sentences of the theoretical language must fulfill in order to have a positive function for

[2] For logical positivism metaphysics is meaningless. For Popper and his supporters it may be meaningful but it is not scientific. I cannot discuss these differences here.
[3] In sociology there are methodologists who fail to see the point of this distinction. ' . . . Though philosophers of science are generally inclined to admit that there are other concepts [i.e. theoretical in Carnap's sense] in many or most scientific theories. Such concepts are electron, cause, a person's predisposition and the like. We will deal here only with observational concepts.' A. L. Stinchcombe, *Constructing Social Theories* (New York: Harcourt, Brace, & World, 1968) p. 38. These remarks consign science, as far as sociology is concerned, to the humble task of recording and summarising facts, to a level no different in principle from Lullism or from Renaissance variants of the Art of Memory.

the explanation and prediction of observable events and thus to be acceptable as empirically meaningful. ([10] p. 38)

In addition to L_T and L_O we have a theory, T, consisting of a finite number of postulates formulated in L (these are the basic postulates, 'the fundamental laws of science') and correspondence rules which connect the terms of L_T with those of L_O – i.e. a complete interpretation of some of the terms of L_T. As an example of the latter :

. . . a rule might refer to two material bodies u and v (i.e., observable at locations u and v); they must be neither too small nor too large for an observer to see them and to take them into his hands. The rule may connect the theoretical term 'mass' with the observable predicate 'heavier than' as follows : If u is heavier than v, the mass of u is greater than the mass of v. ([10] p. 48)

These rules guarantee the significance of theoretical deductions of conclusions in L_O from premises in L_O :

Since both the premises and the conclusions belong to L_O there can be no objection against the use of correspondence rules and of L_T, as far as the meaningfulness of the results of the derivation procedure is concerned. ([10] p. 47)

Thus some of the theoretical terms acquire empirical significance directly through their connection with observational terms via the correspondence rules. The remaining terms are connected with the first ones through the postulates of T. We can now consider what is required for a theoretical term to be empirically meaningful. Roughly (the details do not concern us here), it means that an assumption about, e.g. the magnitude M, makes a difference for the prediction of an observable event. That is, given T and the correspondence rules, there must be an observation sentence that can be deduced from a theoretical sentence in which M is the only term of L_T and some additional assumptions. It must not be deducible from the additional assumptions alone. If the theoretical terms appearing in these assumptions are known to be empirically meaningful, it then follows that M must be meaningful also. Thus, the terms of L_T must be examined for significance in a serial order. The first terms to be examined must be such that they can be shown to be significant without presupposing the significance of other theoretical terms. This will be the case for those terms which are directly connected with L_O by the correspondence rules. Criteria for the significance of theoretical sentences can be constructed along similar lines.

Carnap provides as rigorous a formulation as possible of the logical empiricist criteria for the empirical significance of theoretical terms and sentences. A statement that is significant can be tested against observation, that is, in principle, against experience. Thus, the criteria for significance allow for the testing of theoretical statements (hypotheses) against the basic and irreducible elements of knowledge, against elements that, in this conception, are thought to be entirely independent of theory. It is on this last condition alone that the empiricist conception of 'testing' can appear to be a necessary and rational moment in the advancement of knowledge. On this condition testing provides grounds for the rejection or provisional acceptance of theory by evaluating it in terms of something that is entirely independent of the theory in question.[4]

Two points are especially significant in Carnap's formulations. First, the definition of significance is obviously relative to T, the fundamental laws of science. Thus, while the class of theoretical terms admitted as empirically significant does not necessarily change whenever a new fact is discovered, it does change 'when a radical revolution in the system of science is made' ([10] p. 51). What changes, in this conception, is not the whole of the language of science but only the theoretical part of it. In this respect Carnap's position is radically distinct from that advanced by Kuhn.[5] For the latter, although his position is somewhat ambiguous in this respect, it appears that L_O changes with each radical revolution in science.

Secondly, it should be noted that the effect of Carnap's criteria of empirical significance is precisely to exclude the practice of

---

[4] It may be noted that the most vociferous advocates of testing as an index of scientificity (Popper and his associates) reject this essential condition under which the empiricist conception of testing becomes an entirely rational procedure, e.g. Popper, *The Logic of Scientific Discovery* (London: Hutchinson, 1959) ch. v.

[5] T. S. Kuhn, *The Structure of Scientific Revolutions*, 2nd ed. (Chicago: Chicago University Press, 1970). On this question see especially Chapters 9 and 10.

assigning empirical indicators to theoretical concepts by means of the more or less arbitrary whim of the investigator. It is worth emphasising this point since what is rigorously excluded by Carnap is characteristic of the vulgar positivism of much methodological writing in the social sciences.[6] Where it does occur the effect of this practice of arbitrarily assigning 'empirical' indicators to 'non-empirical', or theoretical, concepts is to tender rigorous demonstration impossible. At first sight it might seem that Cicourel's and Douglas' critique of sociologists' use of official statistics is directed against this practice. From the point of view of logical empiricism the force of such a critique could hardly be disputed. However, these authors proceed to dispose of the pre-theoretical observation language as well. As a result even the limited forms of proof recognised by logical empiricism must collapse.

It should be added that those rigorous forms of proof and demonstration that are possible and necessary in Carnap's conception (i.e., strict deduction of observable consequences from theoretical statements and their testing) depend upon the existence, at least in principle, of a clear and unambiguous distinction between the theoretical and observational languages. Where this distinction ceases to be entirely clear and unambiguous (e.g., Hempel, Quine, and, in a rather different sense, Popper), testing against a reality that is independent of the theory in question can no longer be guaranteed. To that extent testing itself ceases to be the rational procedure that it is in Carnap's conception. Where the distinction vanishes completely (e.g., Kuhn), the

[6] Is it necessary to cite examples of this tendency? The following texts may suffice: (a) H. M. Blalock, Jr., *Theory Construction* (Englewood Cliffs, N.J.: Prentice-Hall, 1969). 'The essential point is that the auxiliary theory linking the theoretical variables to measured indicators will contain causal assumptions that, in themselves, *can never be tested directly* [my emphasis – in fact, they can never be tested at all]. This means that both the main theory and the auxiliary theory must be combined in order to make definite empirical predictions.' (p. 152) (b) P. F. Lazarsfeld, 'A Conceptual Introduction to Latent Structure Analysis', in Lazarsfeld (ed.), *Mathematical Thinking in the Social Sciences* (Glencoe: The Free Press, 1954). This admirably clear text is concerned with 'how precisely inferences from concrete observations to underlying concepts are to be made' (p. 354). An underlying concept does not exist 'in any tangible sense. It is a construct whose existence is inferred from the manifest data' (p. 371). Latent structures are mathematical or statistical constructs connected to observation terms by arbitrarily chosen types of mathematical functions (e.g. they may be continuous or stochastic, the choice depending on convenience). Once these functions have been chosen then different latent structures may be examined for 'fit' against manifest data. Nevertheless, the choice of function is itself quite arbitrary.

rationality of testing also vanishes completely. Except, that is, in the limited sense that it is one of the rules of the game for that form of life called science : it is one of the things that distinguishes science from cricket or gardening.[7] Even this limited 'rationality' vanishes in the case of scientific revolutions, since L_0 itself is transformed and the new and old paradigms are radically incomparable.

(ii) *Inadequacy of These Conceptions*

Unfortunately, for all the rigour that Carnap wrings out of the empiricist conception of knowledge, scientific experimentation is never reducible to some empiricist process of testing theory against essentially pre-theoretical observation. Still less is scientific knowledge reducible to human experience; nor, for that matter, are the pre-scientific knowledges that are produced by theoretical ideologies. I have attempted to demonstrate in Chapter 3 of this text that a particular form of knowledge, namely official statistics, is in no way reducible to the subjective experiences of enumerators and other officials. On the contrary, all such statistics are the product of a determinate process of production of knowledge governed by a determinate system of concepts (it is by no means necessary that this system be coherent).

These points cannot be elaborated here. The reader is referred to the works cited in the Bibliography. For present purposes a simple illustration must suffice. We take the example of what might appear to be an observational category, time, with particular reference to Galileo's law of fall.[8] In order to compare the rates of fall of light and heavy bodies – according to Galilean mechanics, they are identical in a vacuum – or to measure the acceleration due to gravity, it is necessary to have the means of measuring time, that is, reliable clocks. The motion of a pendulum appears to offer the ideal instrument for constructing such a time-piece, since the period of small oscillations remains constant even where its motion is continuously retarded by air

[7] This effectively reduces the rationalist forms of proof and demonstration of a given science into material suitable for a history of ideas or a sociology of knowledge. See Schutz's account of science as one finite province of meaning amongst many others, 'On Multiple Realities' [34], 1962, pp. 207–59, and [12] pp. 34–8. Schutz's positions are examined in [23].

[8] This exposition follows that of Koyré in 'An Experiment in Measurement' [24] pp. 89–117.

resistance and no two oscillations are identical. It only remains to determine the period of oscillation of a pendulum and to construct one of a suitable length. Two attempts at such a determination, both relatively successful, are of interest. The second attempt to be discussed resulted in the precise experimental determination of g (the acceleration due to gravity).

The first attempt to be examined here was made in Italy by a team of Jesuits led by Riccioli, well-known in the history of the sciences for his attempts to refute Copernicus. He established the period of a pendulum by counting its oscillations over a period of time known by the motion of the stars, for example, over a sidereal day. The team of Jesuits were used to maintain the pendular motion against air resistance by giving a new push after a certain number of beats – this pushing is by no means easy and requires considerable training – and to count the number of beats over the full time period. After many trials he succeeded in constructing a pendulum with a period of just under one second (59·36′′′). The number of oscillations can be translated into seconds by means of tables, and a human clock can be constructed. Riccioli trained two of his collaborators,

> gifted not only for physics but also for music, to count *un, de, tre*. . . . (in the Bolognese dialect in which these words are shorter than in Italian) in a perfectly regular and uniform way, as are wont to do those who direct the execution of musical pieces, in such a way that to the pronunciation of each figure corresponded an oscillation of the pendulum. ([24] p. 106)

The construction of this clock cannot be considered to be independent of theory. In addition to the recognition that the period of small oscillations is constant, it requires, in particular, the astronomical knowledge involved in the precise determination of the passage through the meridian line of the Spica to that of Arcturus, and the knowledge that this passage takes 3192 seconds.

Huygens, on the other hand, was able to construct a mechanical clock that keeps better time than Riccioli's and which embodies in its construction the laws of Galilean dynamics. This clock was the product of his theoretical investigations of the characteristics of circular and oscillatory motion. In addition, it required the determination of the isochronous curve (the cycloid) and the discovery of means to constrain the bob of a pendulum to follow this curve. Huygens solved both of these problems by means of his development of the theory of the evolutes of geometical curves. His formula for the period of a pendulum ($T = \pi \sqrt{1/g}$) determines g as a function of the length and the period of the pendulum. Accordingly Huygens established the value of g as $\dfrac{981 \text{ cm}}{\text{sec}^2}$, the value that has been accepted ever since. In thus constructing an accurate and reliable time-piece, Huygens made it possible to determine the speed of fall and, therefore, made possible the determination of g through the motion of falling bodies. The theoretical advances that made this measurement possible (the theory of pendular motion) also rendered it unnecessary.

Koyré concludes that :

The meaning and value of the Huygensian circuit is therefore clear : not only are good experiments based upon theory, but even the means to perform them are nothing else than theory incarnate. ([24] p. 113)

In these examples the measurement of time is a theoretical operation. It cannot be reduced to the language of 'total momentary experience' or to any pre-theoretical physical object language. It requires no correspondence rules connecting it to some allegedly pre-theoretical elements of knowledge to determine its empirical significance. That significance is a determination of the place and function of time in the problematic of the new mechanics. Need I add that Riccioli's clock is perfectly adequate and reliable up to a certain level of precision and, further, that to make use of its readings does not require reference to the 'meanings' or 'background expectancies' of its Jesuit components; and that, finally, its inadequacy beyond a certain level of precision is not an effect of the consciousnesses of these individuals (who could be replaced without loss by suitably trained atheists, police officers or sociology students), but is, in the strictest possible sense, an effect of the theoretical inadequacy of its construction?

BIBLIOGRAPHY

THE works of Cicourel and Douglas discussed in Chapter 2 depend on positions elaborated by Schutz and Garfinkel. Despite its generally anti-theoretical position, Cicourel (1964) contains some acute observations concerning sociologists' use of surveys, questionnaires, attitude scales, etc. Some of Garfinkel's critical observations are similarly acute – especially the paper 'Methodological Adequacy . . .' in Garfinkel (1967). For other examples of this tendency see McHugh (this purports to be an experimental study of how people define situations) and the papers collected in Douglas (1971), Garfinkel and Sacks, and Sudnow. Schutz presents his work as if it were an extension and elaboration of positions developed by Husserl (and, to a lesser extent, by Bergson and James). In fact, it involves a gross vulgarisation and distortion of Husserl's work. For a critique of Schutz and an examination of his relation to Husserl, see Hindess (1972).

Other variants of the subjectivist critique of sociology may be found, for example, in Winch and in symbolic interaction (e.g., Becker, Blumer). Winch argues that the relation between a reason and an action is an internal, logical relation and, consequently, that reasons cannot be considered the causes of actions – since they would not be distinct from their supposed effects. To understand a human action, therefore, is an activity different in kind from the 'causal' analyses that Winch supposes are undertaken in the natural sciences. Winch's philosophical critics (e.g. MacIntyre) adopt somewhat different variants of the same philosophical tendency and argue that actors' reasons can be seen as causes of their actions.

Thorner (1962) contains an extremely useful evaluation of the methods used for the collection of social and economic data in the Census of India, 1951, the Census of Landholding, and

59

other enquiries, and also an examination of changes since the 1880's in the structure of the Indian labour force, and the level of agricultural output. For all the critical value of these texts, Thorner's own position (e.g. 1971) is far from satisfactory.

By far the most rigorous and systematic analyses of agrarian statistics from the point of view of the capitalist transformation of agriculture are to be found in Lenin's studies of the development of capitalist agriculture in Europe and North America. It may be instructive to compare these analyses with Chayanov's use of zemstvo statistics to argue, against the Marxist position, that there had been little differentiation of the peasantry in late 19th and early 20th century Russia. Thorner (1971) follows Chayanov in treating the peasant family farm as the basic unit of a distinctive type of economic system.

I have insisted that the basis of knowledge is not to be found in human 'experience' but in concepts and rationalist forms of proof and demonstration. In particular, that knowledge is never simply given but is always the product of a determinate practice – which may or may not be scientific and may not, as with the bulk of social statistics, be particularly coherent. In this I have followed positions elaborated in Althusser (1970, especially part 6) and Althusser and Balibar (1970, part 1), and the advanced theoretical work of Bachelard, Canguilhem and Koyré in the history of the sciences. Of these last only the work of Koyré is widely available in English translation, but see also Bachelard (1964), especially Chapter 5, 'The Chemistry of Fire : History of a False Problem', and Bachelard (1968) for a systematic refutation of the claims of realism in the natural sciences. Lecourt's text is an excellent short analysis of Bachelard's concepts. Fichant gives a good account of the theory of the history of the sciences.

Carnap (1956) is a relatively non-technical exposition of his later methodological position. For an example of what can be achieved within the limits of this conception see Carnap (1966). For related positions which reject Carnap's rigorous distinction between theoretical and observational languages see, for example. Hempel and Quine. Since the Appendix was concerned solely to indicate the function of 'observational' categories in the methodological discourse of ethnomethodologists and their 'orthodox' opponents, I have not attempted to examine the variants of logical empiricism – examples and a bibliography may be found in Ayer. Classical texts for this tendency are by Mach and Duhem. Koyré (1956) is a useful critical examination of one positivist history of science.

I have assumed that readers will be familiar with the types of positions presented in the standard, positivist texts on research methods or social statistics. The texts of Galtung and of Moser and Kalton may serve as examples.

[1] Althusser, L., *For Marx* (London: Allen Lane, The Penguin Press, 1970).

[2] Althusser, L., and Balibar, E., *Reading Capital* (London: N.L.B., 1970).

[3] Ayer, A. J. (ed.), *Logical Positivism* (London: Allen & Unwin, 1959; Glencoe, Ill.: The Free Press, 1959).

[4] Bachelard, G., *The Philosophy of No* (New York: The Orion Press, 1968).

[5] Bachelard, G., *The Psychoanalysis of Fire* (Boston: Beacon Press, 1964).

[6] Becker, H., 'Becoming a Marihuana User', *American Journal of Sociology*, LIX (November 1953), 235–42.

[7] Blumer, H., 'Sociological Analysis and the "Variable"', *American Sociological Review*, XXI (December 1956), 683–90.

[8] Canguilhem, G., *Etudes d'Histoire et de Philosophie des Sciences* (Paris: J. Vrin, 1968).

[9] Carnap, R., M. Gardner (ed.), *Philosophical Foundations of Physics* (New York and London: Basic Books, 1966).

[10] Carnap, R., 'The Methodological Character of Theoretical Concepts', *Minnesota Studies in the Philosophy of Science*, vol. I (1956) 38–76.

[11] Chayanov, A.V., Thorner D., *et al.* (eds.), *The Theory of Peasant Economy* (Homewood, Ill.: Irwin, 1966).

[12] Cicourel, A. V., *Method and Measurement in Sociology* (Glencoe, Ill.: The Free Press, 1964).

[13] Cicourel, A. V., *The Social Organisation of Juvenile Justice* (New York and London: John Wiley, 1968).

[14] Douglas, J., *The Social Meanings of Suicide* (Princeton, N.J.: Princeton University Press, 1967).

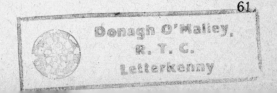

[15] Douglas, J., 'The Sociological Analysis of the Social Meanings of Suicide', *European Journal of Sociology*, VII (1966), 249–75.

[16] Douglas, J. (ed.), *Understanding Everyday Life: Towards the Reconstruction of Sociological Knowledge* (London: Routledge & Kegan Paul, 1971).

[17] Duhem, P., *The Aim and Structure of Physical Theory* (Princeton, N.J.: Princeton University Press, 1954).

[18] Fichant, M., 'L'Idée d'une Histoire des Sciences', in M. Fichant and M. Pecheux, *Sur l'Histoire des Sciences* (Paris: François Maspero, 1969). A substantial portion of this paper has been translated in *Theoretical Practice*, no. 3–4 (1971).

[19] Galtung, J., *Theory and Methods of Social Research* (London: George Allen & Unwin, 1967).

[20] Garfinkel, H., *Studies in Ethnomethodology* (Englewood Cliffs, N.J.: Prentice-Hall, 1967).

[21] Garfinkel, H., and Sacks, H. (eds.), *Contributions to Ethnomethodology* (Bloomington: Indiana University Press, 1972).

[22] Hempel, C. G., 'Empiricist Criteria of Cognitive Significance', in *Aspects of Scientific Explanation* (Glencoe, Ill.: The Free Press, 1965).

[23] Hindess, B., 'The "Phenomenological" Sociology of Alfred Schutz', *Economy and Society*, vol. I, no. 1 (1972), 1–27.

[24] Koyré, A., *Metaphysics and Measurement* (London: Chapman & Hall, 1968).

[25] Koyré, A., *Newtonian Studies* (London: Chapman & Hall, 1965).

[26] Koyré, A., 'The Origins of Modern Science: A New Interpretation', *Diogenes*, no. 16 (Winter 1956), 1–22.

[27] Lecourt, D., *L'Epistémologie Historique de Gaston Bachelard* (Paris: J. Vrin, 1969).

[28] Lenin, V. I., *The Development of Capitalism in Russia; The Agrarian Question and the Critics of Marx; Capitalism and Agriculture in the United States of America*, in vols. III, V, XIII, and XVII respectively of *Collected Works* (London: Lawrence & Wishart, 1960).

[29] Mach, E., *The Analysis of Sensations* (New York: Dover Publications, 1959).

[30] MacIntyre, A., 'The Idea of a Social Science', *Aristotelian Society Supplementary Volume 61* (1967), 95–114.

[31] McHugh, P., *Defining the Situation: The Organization of Meaning in Social Interaction* (Indianapolis: Bobbs-Merrill, 1968).

[32] Moser, C. A., and Kalton, G., *Survey Methods in Social Investigation* (London: Heinemann, 1971).

[33] Quine, W. V. O., 'On What There Is' and 'Two Dogmas of Empiricism', in *From a Logical Point of View* (New York: Harper Torchbooks, 1963).

[34] Schutz, A., *Collected Papers*, 3 vols. (The Hague: Martinus Nijhoff, 1962, 1964, 1966).

[35] Schutz, A., *The Phenomenology of the Social World* (London: Heinemann, 1972).

[36] Sudnow, D. (ed.), *Studies in Interaction* (Glencoe, Ill.: The Free Press, 1971).

[37] Thorner, D. and A., *Land and Labour in India* (London: Asia Publishing House, 1962).

[38] Thorner, D., 'Peasant Economy as a Category in Economic History', in T. Shanin (ed.), *Peasants and Peasant Societies* (Harmondsworth: Penguin Books, 1971).

[39] Winch, P., *The Idea of a Social Science and Its Relation to Philosophy* (London: Routledge & Kegan Paul, 1958).

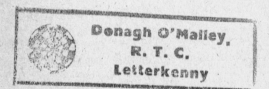